Preparatory Level - Book A

A Playful Path to Essential Music Skills (Ages 4–6)

Jennifer Prado

Founder of Prado Music Academy
Creator of The Prado Piano Method™

The Prado Piano Method™ Piano Curriculum

Preparatory Level – Book A
A Playful Path to Essential Music Skills (Ages 4–6)

The Prado Piano Method™ introduces young beginners to the world of music through a joyful, step-by-step approach that develops five essential musical skills: music theory, sight reading, ear training, technique, and piano repertoire.

Through engaging activities such as rhythm games, note-reading exercises, musical symbol exploration, fun songs, and beginner composing tasks, children build coordination, creativity, and confidence while learning to clap, sing, draw, write, color, compose, and play the piano.

By the end of this book, students will:

Recognize and understand all finger numbers (1–5)
Play simple piano patterns using fingers 2–3–4
Identify and count note values (half notes and quarter notes)
Recognize basic dynamics (f – forte and p – piano)
Perform simple beginner pieces using basic rhythms
Explore creative activities such as drawing, rhythm clapping, and short musical ideas

Book A focuses on building early musical awareness, rhythm understanding, and finger coordination in a playful and supportive way.

The Prado Piano Method™ nurtures a love of music while laying a solid foundation for a lifelong musical journey.

Author's Note:

My approach with young learners is to nurture a genuine love for music through joyful activities and meaningful experiences. This book is designed to inspire and engage young students—making lessons and practice feel playful, creative, and rewarding.

Through imaginative pieces and simple musical games, my goal is to foster curiosity, confidence, and self-expression while building strong musical foundations.

May this book be a helpful companion for teachers and families, guiding children through the delightful first chapter of their musical journey.

— Jennifer P

The Prado Piano Method™

For Teachers and Parents

The **Prado Piano Method™** is designed to introduce young children to piano through joyful exploration, creativity, and structured learning. Each lesson integrates five essential areas of musical development:

Music Theory
Sight Reading
Ear Training
Technique
Piano Repertoire

These elements work together to help students develop strong musical foundations while maintaining curiosity and enjoyment.

Lessons in this book include a variety of engaging activities such as rhythm games, note-reading exercises, musical symbol exploration, and beginner piano pieces. Students are encouraged to clap, sing, draw, write, compose, and play as part of their learning experience.

For young beginners, short and frequent practice sessions are most effective. Teachers and parents are encouraged to support students by celebrating small achievements and creating a positive and encouraging musical environment.

Above all, the goal of **The Prado Piano Method™** is to help children develop a lasting love for music while building confidence and essential musical skills.

This book is part of **The Prado Piano Method™ Piano Curriculum**, a structured series designed to guide students from their first musical experiences to confident piano playing.

The Prado Piano Method™

Preparatory Level – Book A

A Playful Path to Essential Music Skills (Ages 4–6)

THIS BOOK IS LOVED BY:

Table of Contents

Hello Song

Hello __________, how are you today?
(Student Name)

Hello __________, how are you today?
(Student Name)

Very well, thank you.
I'm ready to start
my piano class.

Very well, thank you.
I'm ready to start
my piano class.

*Teachers sing and play the Hello Song before each lesson. Students are encouraged to clap and sing along!

7

Piano Registers: Mr. Bear and His Friends

We are going to embark on a fun musical journey. Are you ready?

Once upon a time, there was a big, friendly bear strolling through the forest.
(Teachers will play low sounds on the piano to imitate the bear's steps.)

He was searching for food for a delicious breakfast. Suddenly, some bushes rustled, and he found a little yellow bird.

"Good morning, little bird!" Mr. Bear said.
(Teachers will play random low notes on the piano to mimic the sound of the bear's voice.)

"Good morning, Mr. Bear!" chirped the happy little bird. "What are you doing here so early in the morning?"
(Teachers will play random high notes on the piano to mimic the little bird's voice.)

"I'm looking for something to eat because I haven't had breakfast yet," said Mr. Bear.
(Teachers will play low notes to mimic the bear's voice.)

"Oh! I know where you can find delicious bananas. Please follow me!"
(Teachers will play high notes on the piano to mimic the little bird's voice.)

Mr. Bear and the little bird set off to find the banana tree and came across two playful monkeys jumping around it.

"Good morning, monkeys!" Mr. Bear said. "We're looking for something to eat."

"Good morning, Mr. Bear and little bird!"
(Teachers will play random notes in the middle register of the piano to mimic the monkeys' voices.)

"Can you help us get some bananas from the tree, please?"
(Teachers play low sounds)

"Absolutely! There's a banana tree!"
(Teachers will play notes in the middle register of the piano to mimic the monkeys' voices.)

The monkeys happily shared the bananas, and from that day on, the bear, the bird, and the monkeys became the best of friends, always playing music and sharing breakfast together in the forest.

***Teachers will read the story and play sounds on the piano in three different registers—low, middle, and high—to imitate the animals' sounds.**

Piano Registers Game

For this game:

- Listen carefully! Circle the animal that matches the sound you hear. Your teacher will play the sounds first.

Close your eyes and guess which animal sound your teacher is playing.
(The teacher will play sounds for Mr. Bear, the little bird, or the monkeys.)

Optional: Play it back! *(Repeat 3 times.)*

Now it's your turn to be the teacher! Play the sounds for Mr. Bear, the little bird, or the monkeys and ask your teacher to guess! *(Repeat 3 times.)*

Would you like to create your own animal or princess story and play the sounds on the piano?

The Piano Posture: Princess or Prince Position

Welcome, Princess/Prince _________________________ **, to our music story!**

(Student Name)

When a princess or prince sits at the piano, they have a very straight back. Can I see yours?

Are you a princess or a prince? Circle the one that shows you!

Let's practice the correct piano sitting position together!

Hand Position: The Little Ball Game

Let's pretend we are holding a little ball in our hands. Place your hands on the keys just like in the image below. Your teacher will also demonstrate. Repeat this exercise three times, and color in a star below with your favorite color each time you try it!

 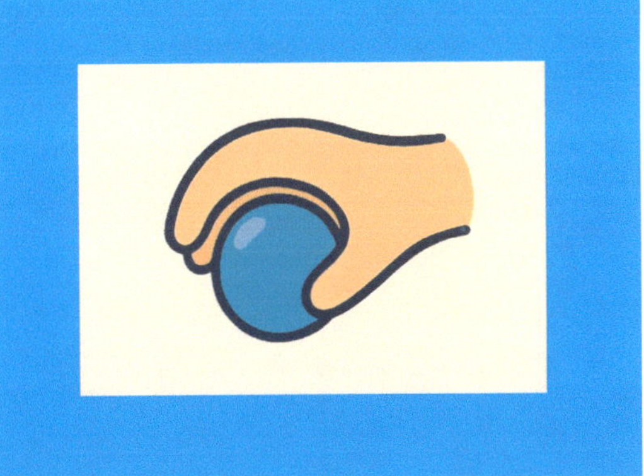 

Finger Numbers: 1-2-3-4-5

Each finger has its own number. Let's find them!

• Trace your hands using your favorite color and add a number on each finger.

• Say hello to each finger by playing them one by one on the piano. Your teacher will help you play each finger by itself.

L.H

R.H

Finger Numbers: The Game

Play any note on the piano using the finger number your teacher points to in the picture. Don't forget to use the correct hand!

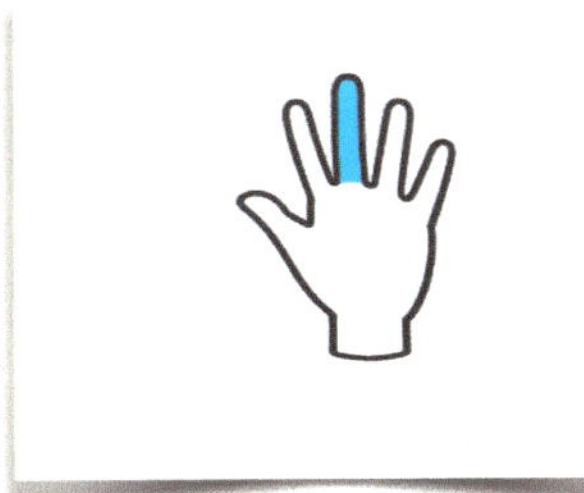    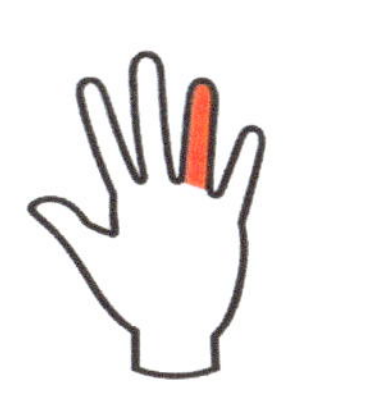

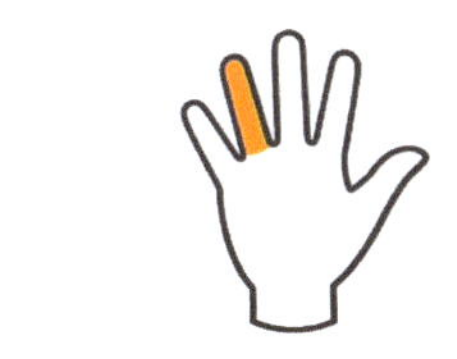 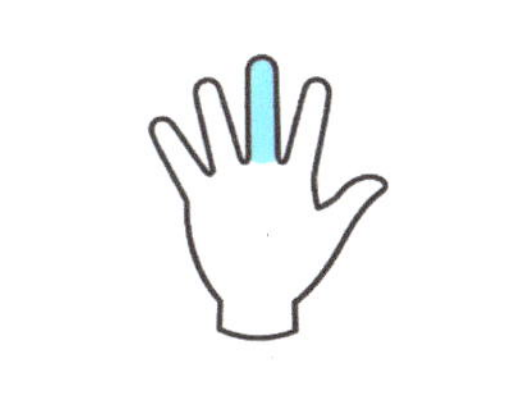   

Now it's your turn! Try creating a song using this order:

R.H : 1 - 5 - 4 - 3 - 2 - 2 - 3 - 3 - 3 - 2 - 5 - 1

L.H : 1 - 5 - 4 - 3 - 2 - 2 - 3 - 3 - 3 - 2 - 5 - 1

Now try creating a song using your own order:

R.H :

L.H :

Black Key Pattern: 2 and 3 Game

For this song:

- Let's find all the groups of two black keys! Now play them with fingers 2 and 3 on each hand. The left hand (L.H.) will play the groups going up the keyboard, and the right hand (R.H.) will play the groups going down..
- Now let's find all the groups of three black keys! Can you play them by yourself? The left hand (L.H.) will play the groups going up the keyboard, while the right hand (R.H.) will play them going down.
- Circle the groups of two black keys in red and the groups of three black keys in blue.

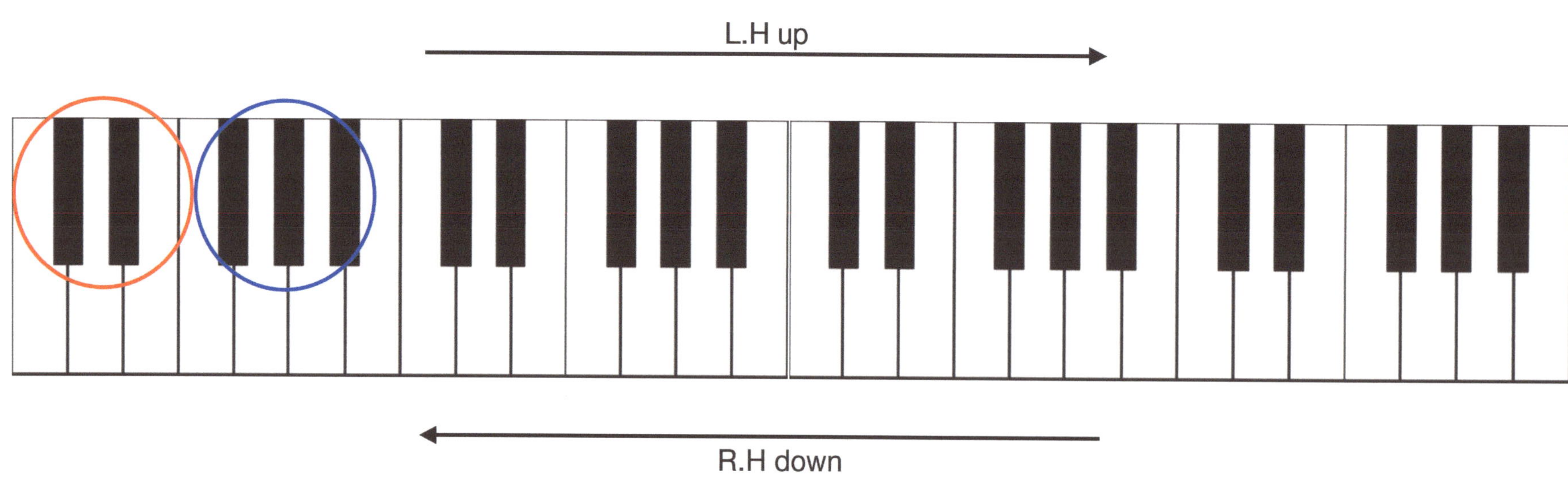

Black Key Song: Your First Song

For this song:

- **Playing on the Picture of the Book!** Using finger number 2 on both hands, play the black keys on the picture of the book, pretending it's a piano. Use your left hand (L.H.) to play going up and your right hand (R.H.) to play going down. Make sure your finger is rounded and curved.
- **Playing on the Piano!** Using finger 2 on both hands, play each black key one by one. Use your left hand (L.H.) to play going up and your right hand (R.H.) to play going down. Make sure your finger is rounded and curved, and play with a steady beat.
- **Can you sing and play at the same time?** Sing the pattern **2–2–2–2–2** going up and **2–2–2–2–2** going down while playing the black keys with finger 2 on both hands. Teachers can accompany the student using the same pattern on the piano.

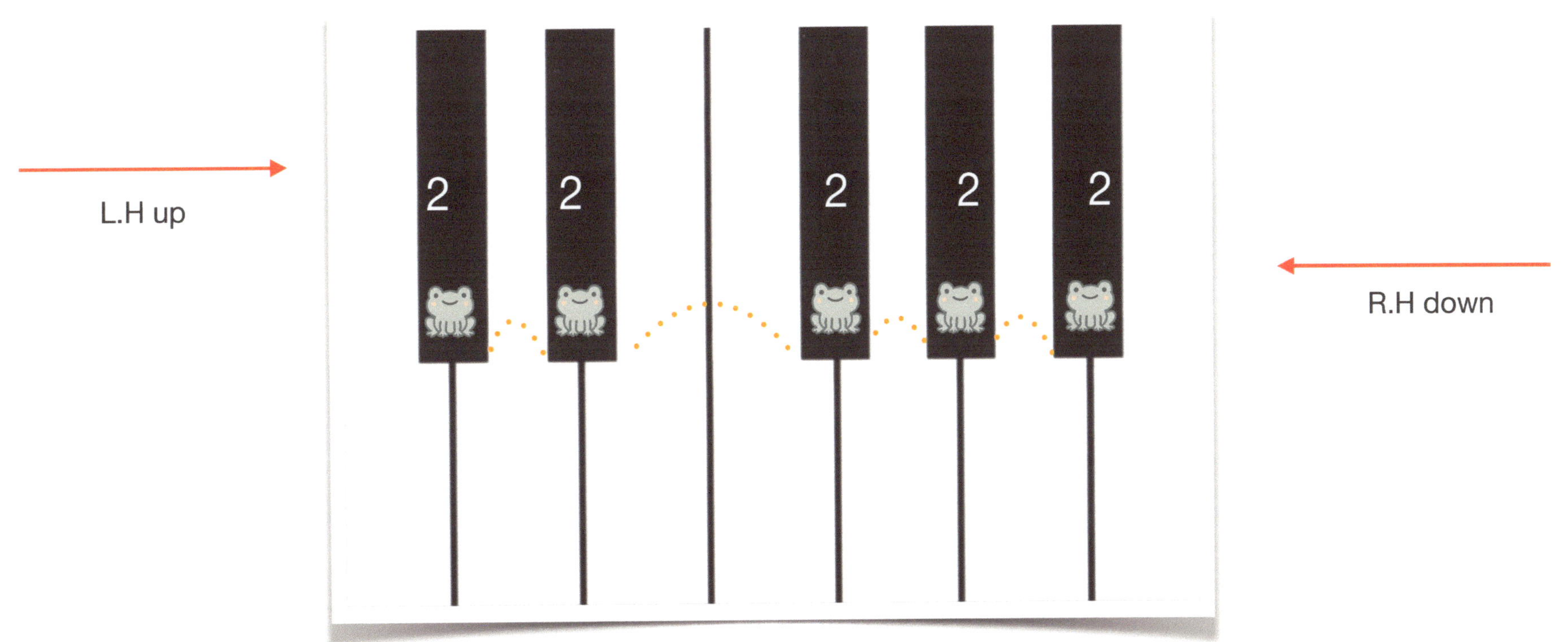

Black Key Song: The Game

For this song:

- As quickly as you can, point out all the groups of 2 black keys in the pictures below and circle them using your favorite color.
- Now, point out all the groups of 3 black keys in the pictures below and circle them using a different color.
- Your teacher will now point to each picture one by one, and your task is to find and play the corresponding black key group on the piano as quickly as you can!
- Would you like to be the teacher? Point to each picture one by one, and your teacher will find them on the piano for you! Yay!
- Let's compose a song together! Using finger number 2, play the groups that your teacher points to. You can use your right hand, left hand, or switch between both hands. Have fun and enjoy making music!

Little Ants

For this song:

- The teacher will first play and sing the song for the student.
- Clap the counts and say the words aloud.
- Use finger 2 on the right hand (R.H.) and practice the movement of the finger on the closed lid of the piano.
- Play each pattern on the group of two black keys with finger 2 on the R.H., moving up each time the pattern appears.
- Sing and play the song.
- Each time you play it, shade one star using your favorite color.

Play this piece 3 times and color a star each time you play!

J. Prado

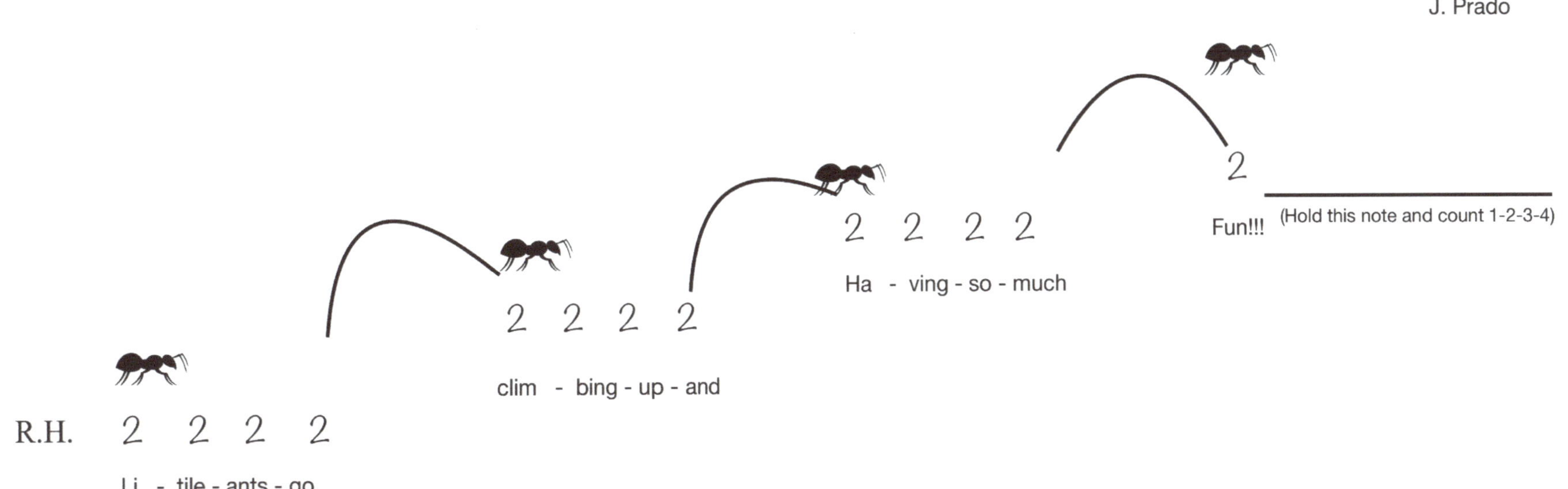

Jumpy Bunny

For this song:

- The teacher will first play and sing the song for the student.
- Tap on your knees to the counts and say the words aloud.
- Use finger 2 on the left hand (L.H.) and practice the movement of the fingers on the closed lid of the piano.
- Use the group of two black keys with fingers 2-3 on the L.H., playing each pattern and moving down every time the pattern appears.
- Sing and play the song.
- Each time you play it, please shade one star using your favorite color.

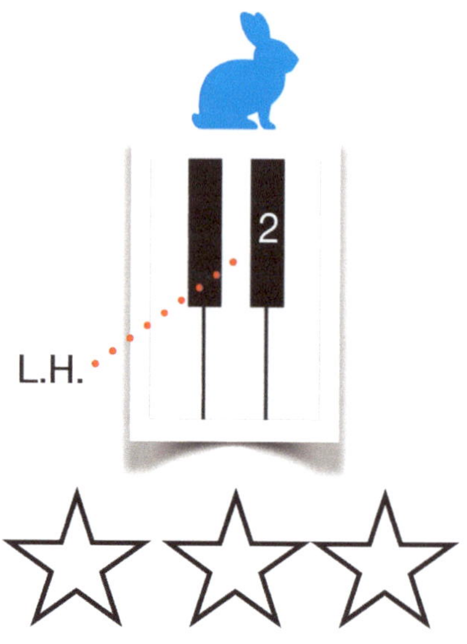

Play this piece 3 times and color a star each time you play!

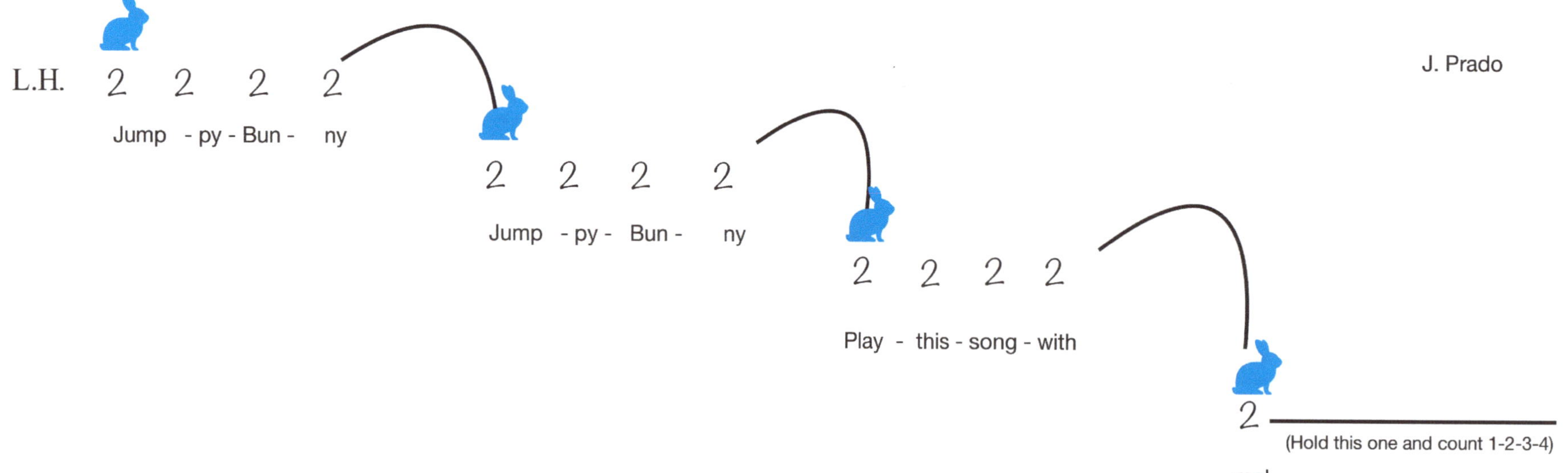

The Mouse and The Cat

For this song:

- The teacher will first play and sing the song for the student.
- Tap on the closed piano lid with the correct hand and say the words aloud.
- Use finger 2 on each hand and practice the movement of the fingers on the closed lid of the piano.
- Use finger 2 on both hands to play the 2-black-key groups: one in the middle and one below!
- Sing and play the song.
- Each time you play it, please shade one star using your favorite color.

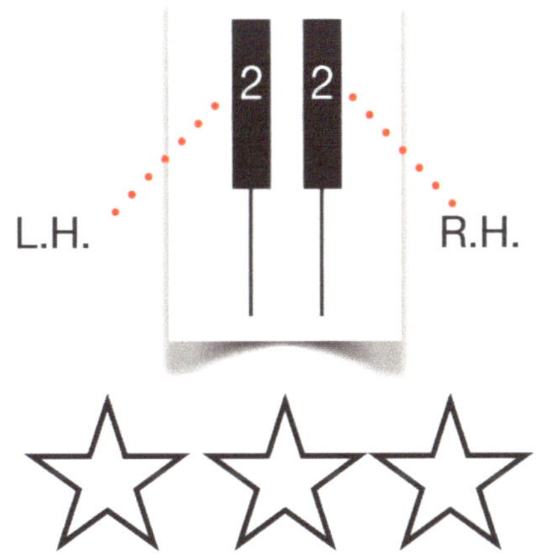

Play this piece 3 times and color a star each time you play!

J. Prado

R.H. 2 2 2 2
Li - ttle - mouse - and

2 2 2 2 2
(Hold this note and count 1-2-3-4)

L.H. 2 2 2 2
Li - ttle - cat - are

2 2 2 2 2
Play - ying - in - their   House!
(Hold this note and count 1-2-3-4)

DOUBLE BAR LINE

Happy Morning Song

For this song:

- The teacher will first play and sing the song for the student.
- Clap the counts and say the words aloud.
- Use fingers 2-3-4 on the right hand (R.H.) and practice the movement of the fingers on the closed lid of the piano.
- Use the group of three black keys with fingers 2-3-4 on the R.H., playing each pattern and moving up every time the pattern appears.
- Sing and play the song.
- Each time you play it, please shade one star using your favorite color.

Play this piece 3 times and color a star each time you play!

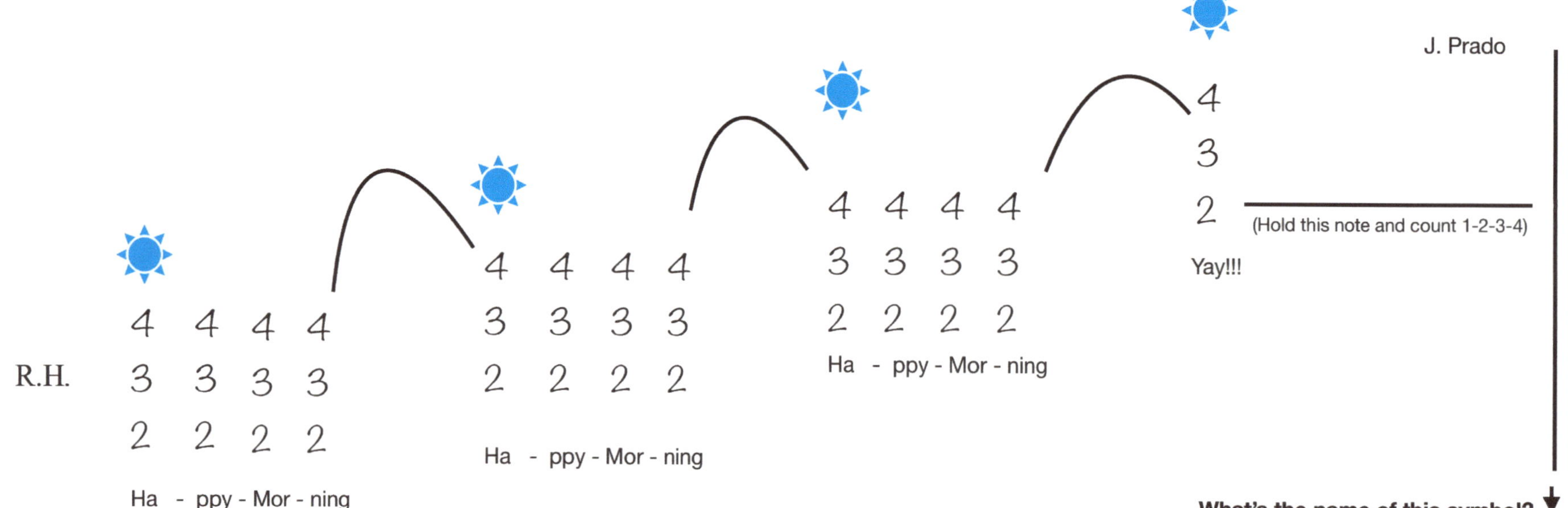

20

Good Night Song

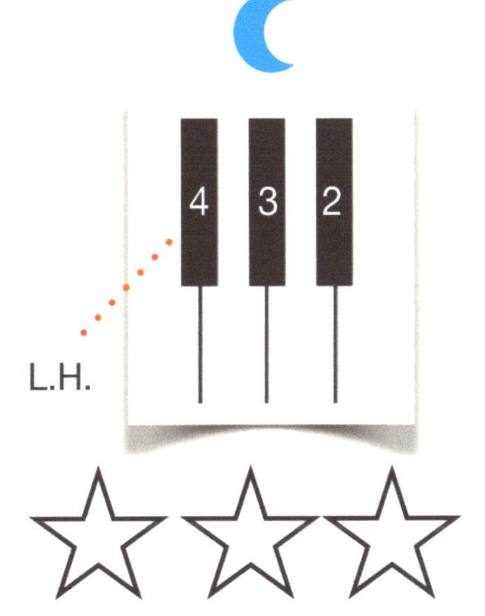

Play this piece 3 times and color a star each time you play!

For this song:

- The teacher will first play and sing the song for the student.
- Tap on your knees to the counts and say the words aloud.
- Use fingers 2-3-4 on the left hand (L.H.) and practice the movement of the fingers on the closed lid of the piano.
- Use the group of three black keys with fingers 2-3-4 on the L.H., playing each pattern and moving down every time the pattern appears.
- Sing and play the song.
- Each time you play it, please shade one star using your favorite color.

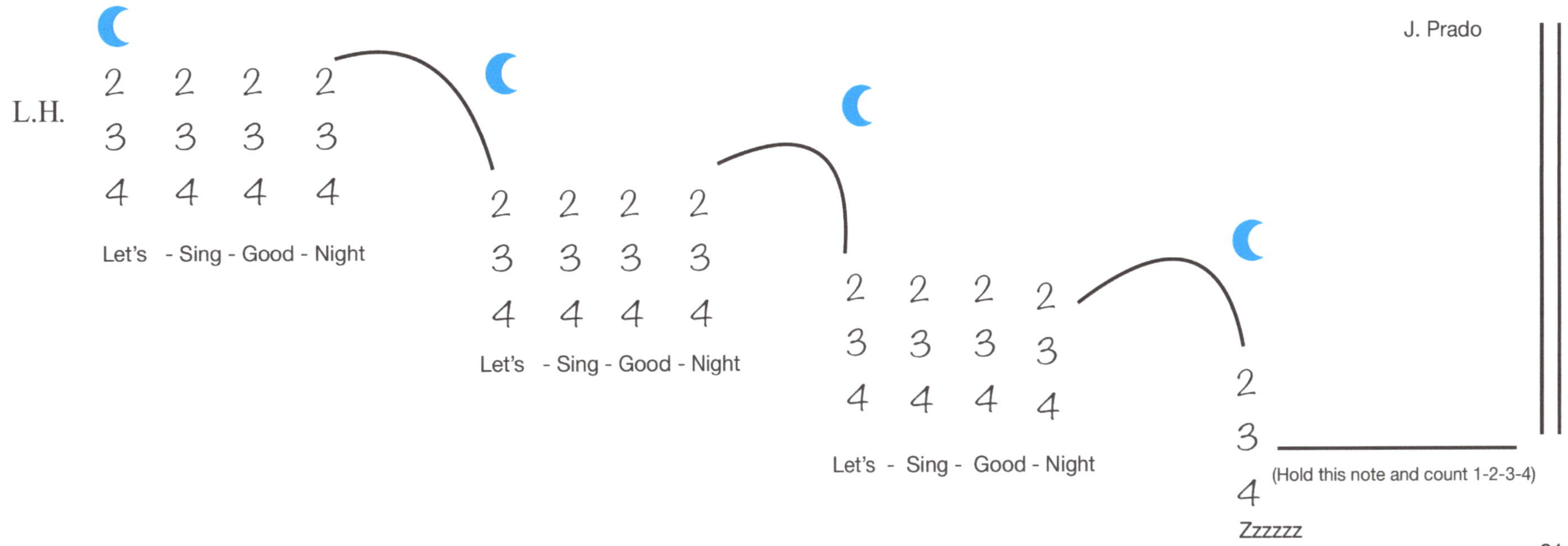

21

1-2-3-Clap

For this song:

- The teacher will first play and sing the song for the student.
- Tap on the piano bench with the correct hand and say the words aloud.
- What do we have that's new in this piece? A repeat sign! That means we play the piece again from the beginning!
- Use fingers 2 and 3 on each hand to practice the movement of the fingers on the closed lid of the piano.
- Use the group of two black keys in the middle of the piano, playing with fingers 2 and 3 on both hands. Remember to repeat the piece twice, as we have a repeat sign!
- Sing and play the song.
- Each time you play it, please shade one star using your favorite color.

Play this piece 3 times and color a star each time you play!

J. Prado

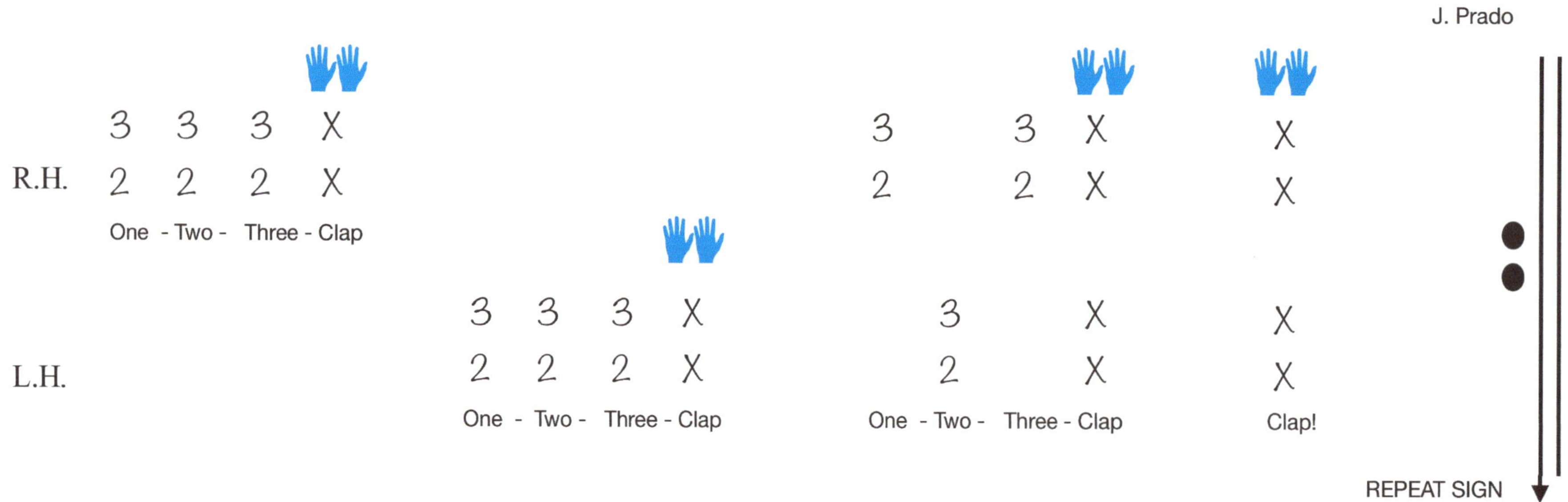

Let's Compose a Song

For this song:

- Using fingers 2 and 3, let's compose a song together.
- Pick the hand that will start.
- Write the numbers for the right hand (R.H.) and left hand (L.H.).
- Would you like to add some words?
- Trace the double bar line
- Let's play the song!

Play this piece 3 times and color a star each time you play!

R.H.

L.H.

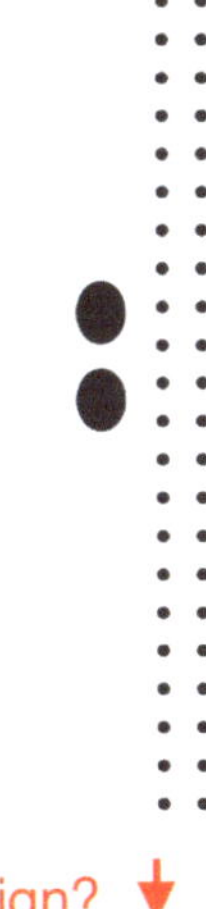

What's the name of this sign? ↓

Dynamics: Meet Our Friend Forte

_f_ = loud

For this game:

- Say the word **'Forte'** in a big, strong voice! Say it three times.
- Play any key on the piano **Forte** (loudly) in different registers of the piano.
- Color the lion using your favorite colors.

Dynamics: Meet Our Friend Piano

$$p = \text{soft}$$

For this game:

- Say the word '**piano**' in a whisper.
- Play any key on the piano **piano** (softly), trying different registers.
- Color the little mouse using your favorite colors.

Dynamics: Let's play with Our friends F and p

For this game:

- The teacher will play a melody on the piano either forte or piano. The student will listen carefully and circle the correct answer - using red for forte, and blue for piano.
- Now, you can be the teacher! Play any key on the piano either forte or piano, and the teacher will point to the correct letter.

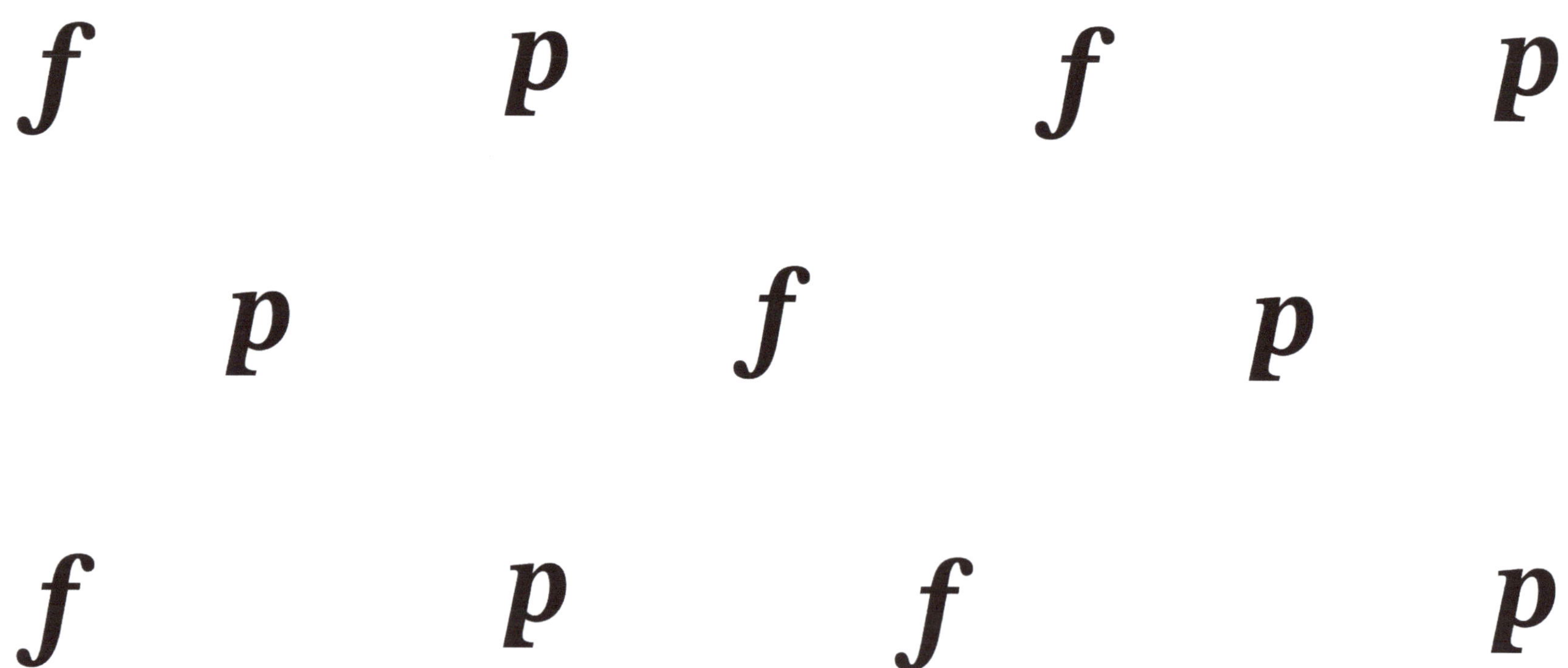

Dinosaur Band

For this song:

- The teacher will first play and sing the song for the student.
- Tap on the closed piano lid using the correct hand and say the words aloud.
- Use fingers 2, 3, and 4 on the left hand (L.H.) and practice the finger movements on the closed lid of the piano.
- Play the group of three black keys in the middle of the piano using fingers 2, 3, and 4 on the left hand (L.H.). Remember to play *forte*!
- Sing and play the song.
- Shade one star with your favorite color each time you play the song.

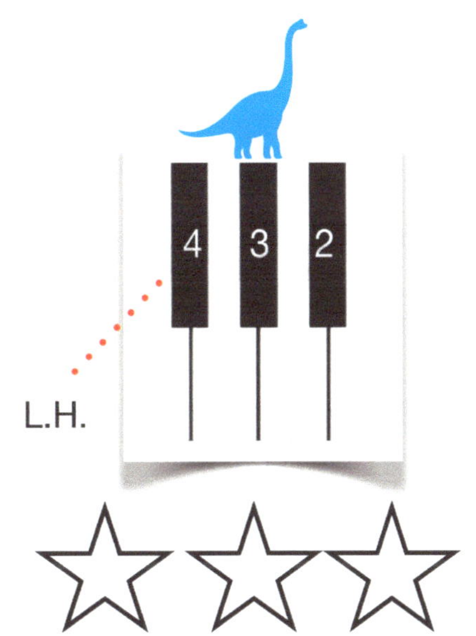

Play this piece 3 times and color a star each time you play!

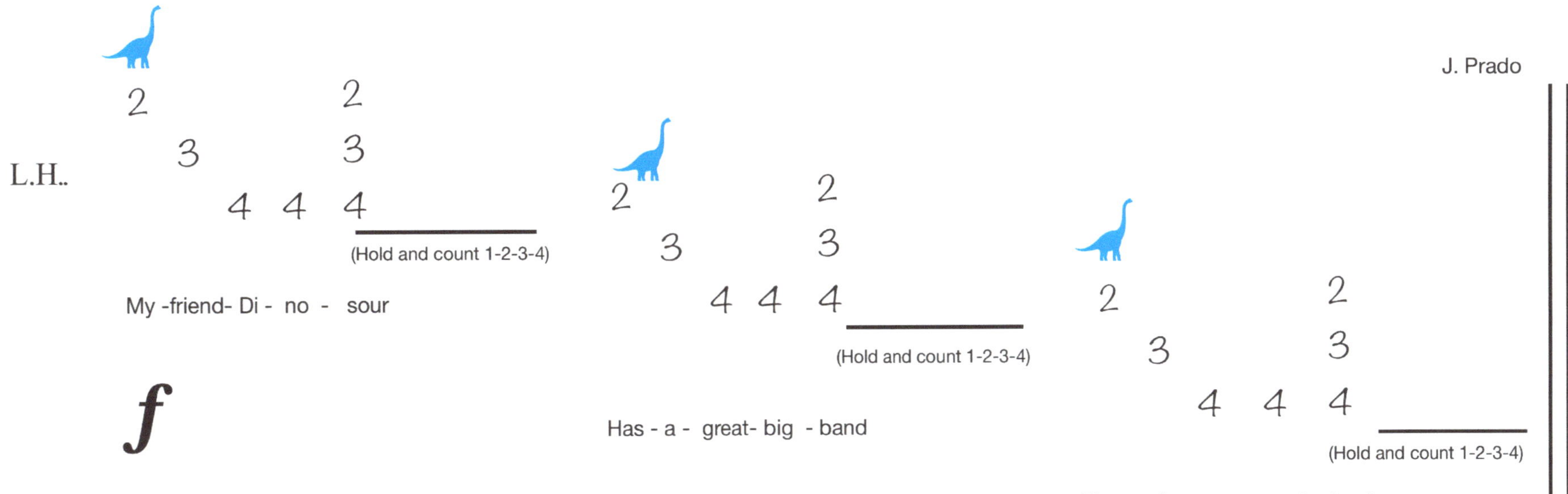

Owl's Song

For this song:

- The teacher will first play and sing the song for the student.
- Tap on the piano bench using the correct hand and say the finger numbers aloud.
- Practice using fingers 2, 3, and 4 on both the right hand (R.H.) and left hand (L.H.) by tapping the closed lid of the piano.
- Play the group of three black keys starting in the middle of the piano with fingers 2, 3, and 4 on the right hand (R.H.), and then use the group of three black keys lower on the piano with the left hand (L.H.). Remember to play forte and piano.
- Shade one star using your favorite color each time you play the song.

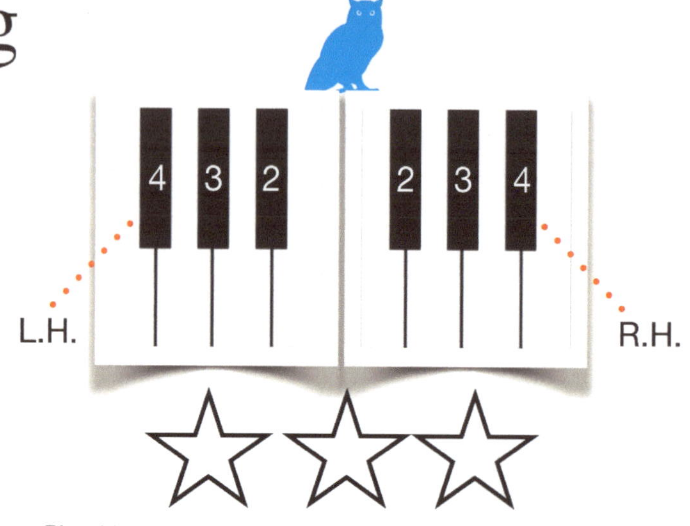

Play this piece 3 times and color a star each time you play!

J. Prado

R.H.

4 3 2 3 4 3 2 ___ (Hold and count 1-2)

p

The - owl- sings - a - tune - at - night

4 3 2 ___ (Hold and count 1-2) Whoo! ***f***

4 3 2 ___ (Hold and count 1-2) Whoo!

4 3 2 ___ (Hold and count 1-2-3-4) Whoo!

L.H.

2 3 4 3 2 3 4 ___ (Hold and count 1-2)

p

Un -der - neath- the - moon's - soft - light.

4 3 2 ___ (Hold and count 1-2) Whoo! ***f***

4 3 2 ___ (Hold and count 1-2) Whoo!

4 3 2 ___ (Hold and count 1-2-3-4) Whoo!

Mary Had a Little Lamb

For this song:

- The teacher will first play and sing the song for the student.
- Tap on the closed piano lid using the correct hand and say the finger numbers aloud.
- Use fingers 2, 3, and 4 on both hands and practice the movements on the closed lid of the piano.
- Play the group of three black keys starting in the middle of the piano with fingers 2, 3, and 4 on the right hand (R.H.). Then, play the group of three black keys lower on the piano with the left hand (L.H.).
- Each time you play the song, shade one star using your favorite color.

Play this piece 3 times and color a star each time you play!

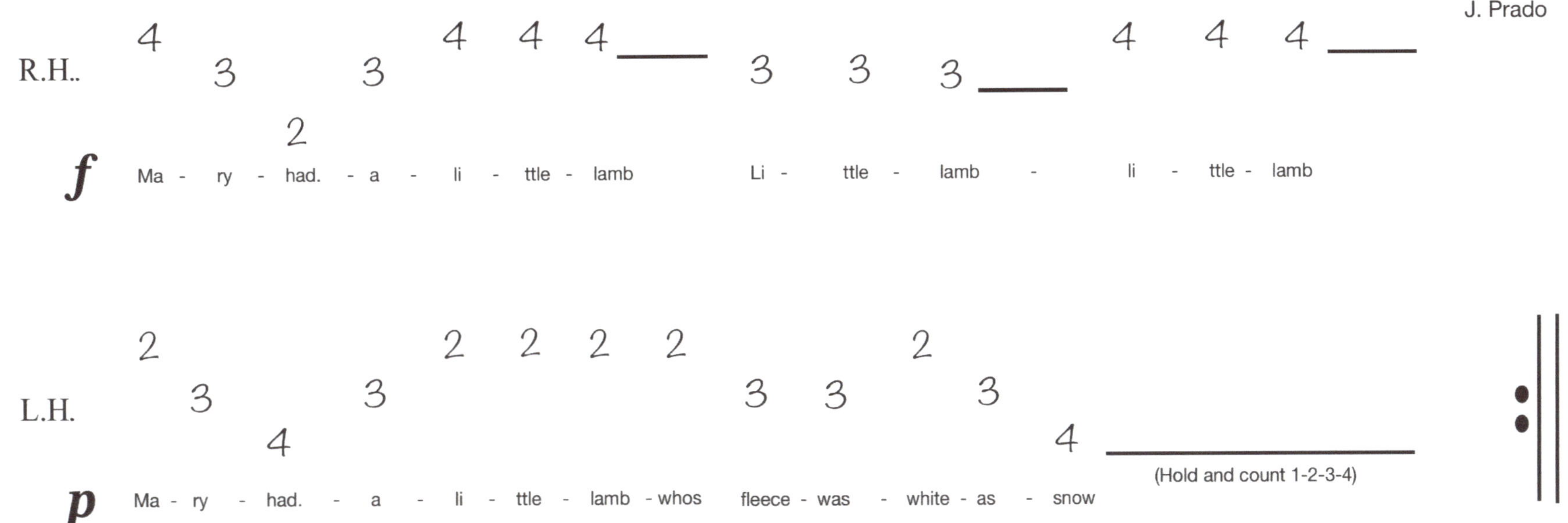

Lest's Compose a Song using F and p

For this song:

- Using fingers 2, 3, and 4, let's compose a song together.
- Choose which hand will start.
- Write the finger numbers for the right hand (R.H.) and left hand (L.H.).
- Let's add dynamics!
- Trace the double bar line at the end of the song. Would you like to add a repeat sign to your piece?
- Now, let's play the song!

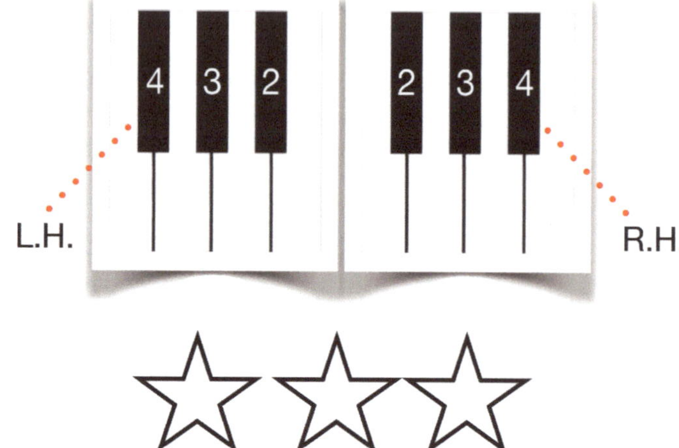

Play this piece 3 times and color a star each time you play!

R.H..

L.H..

Rhythm Friends: Quarter Note

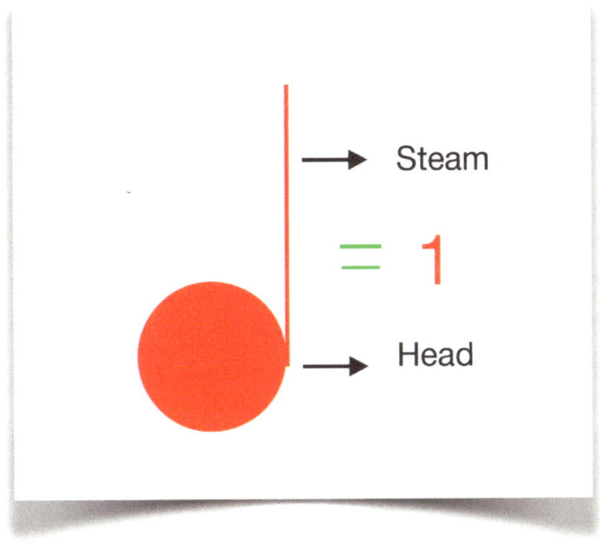

Meet Our Friend, Quarter Note!

Quarter Note gets 1 count or beat. Let's create one together!

- **Make a Circle:** Draw a small circle.
- **Color It In:** Fill in the circle completely.
- **Add a Stem:** Draw a straight line extending upward from the right side of the circle
- **Say Hi:** Wave and say "Hi" to your new quarter note!

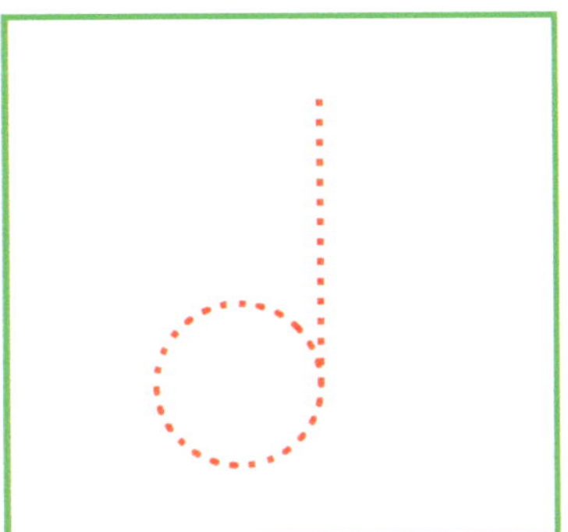
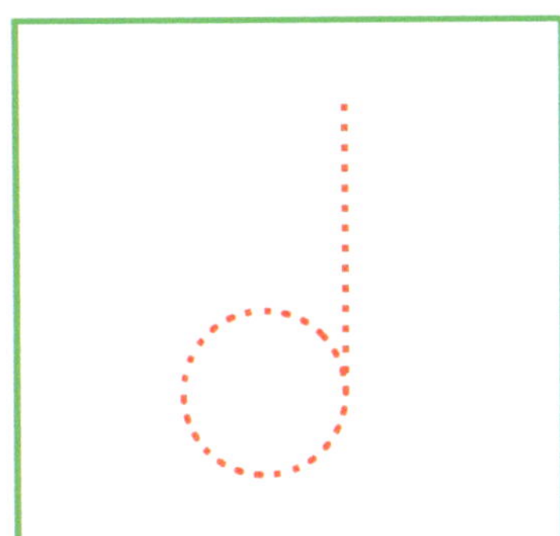
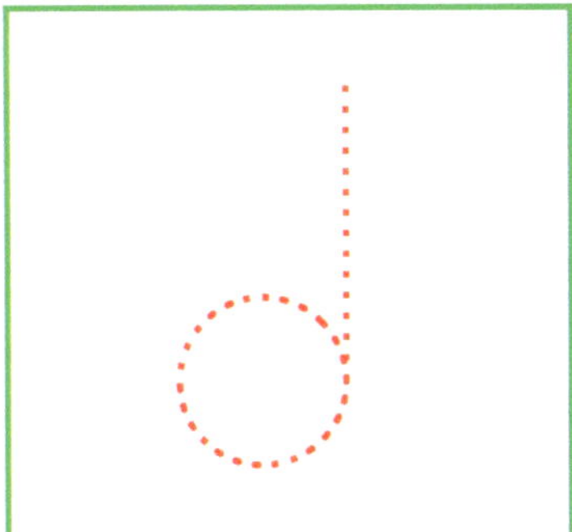

Rhythm Friends: Quarter Note

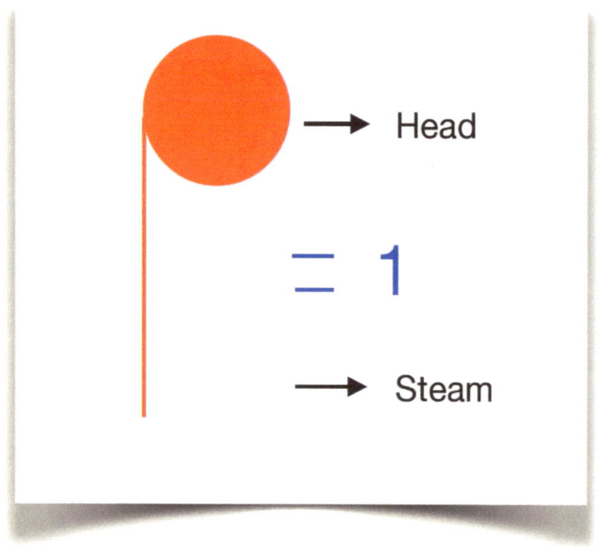

Quarter Note can have the stem going up or down. Let's create one with the stem going down!

- **Make a Circle:** Draw a small circle.
- **Color It In:** Fill in the circle completely.
- **Add a Stem:** Draw a straight line extending downwards from the circle.
- **Say Hi:** Wave and say "Hi" to your new quarter note!

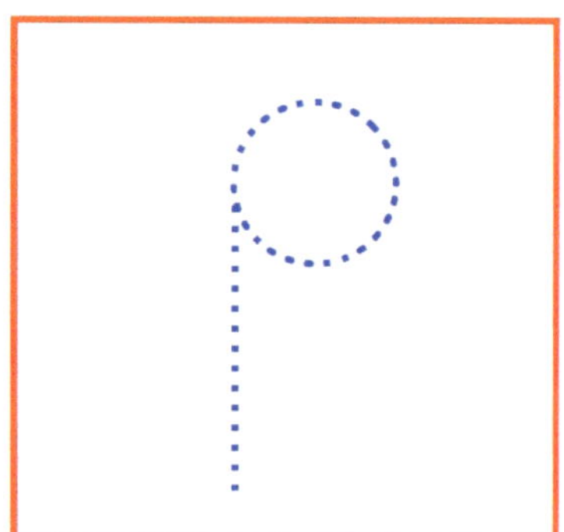
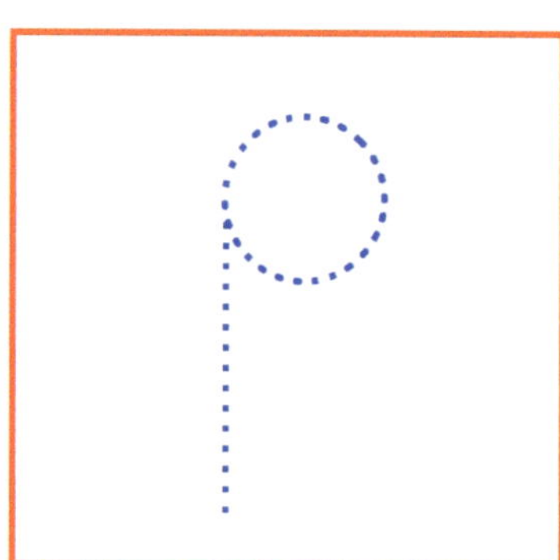
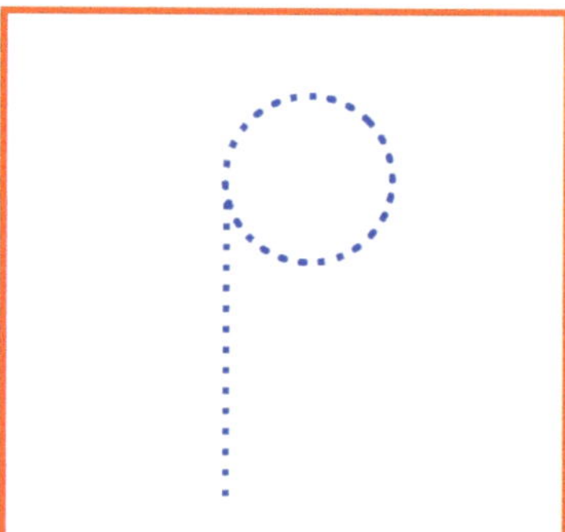

Quarter Note: Game Time Fun

For this game:

- Using the color blue, circle all the quarter notes with the stem UP.
- Using the color red, circle all the quarter notes with the stem DOWN.
- Which hand do you use to play the quarter notes with the stem DOWN?
- Tap the quarter notes using the correct hand. Do this 3 times, each time getting faster, and shade one star each time.

Tap this rhythm 3 times and color a star each time you tap!

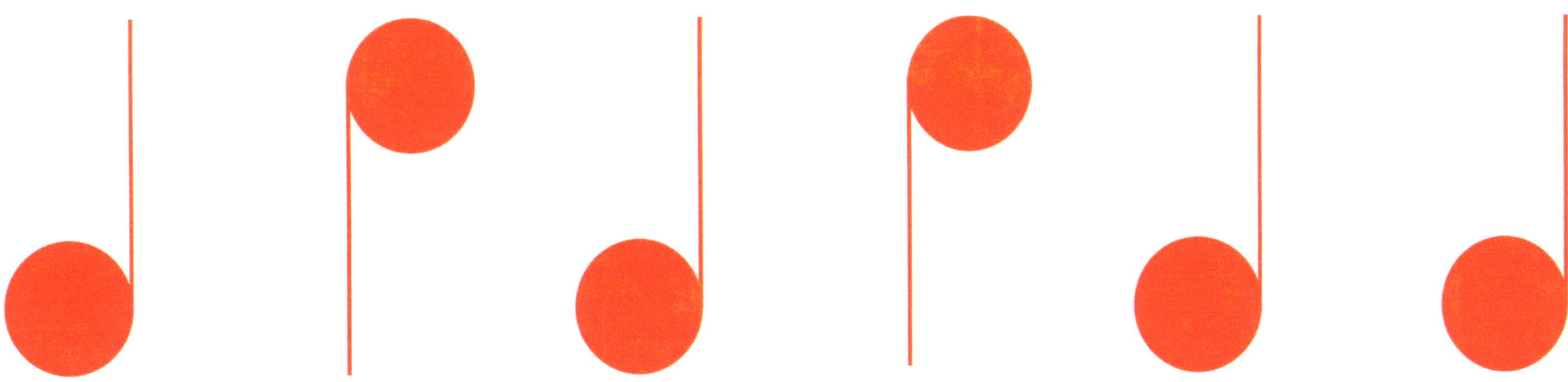

Quarter Note March

For this piece:

- The teacher will first play and sing the song for the student.
- Tap on the closed piano lid with the correct hand while counting the beats aloud.
- Practice the finger movements for each hand separately on the closed lid.
- Use the group of three black keys in the middle of the piano, using fingers 2, 3, and 4 for your right hand (R.H.) and a lower group of three black keys for your left hand (R.H.)
- Add dynamics!
- Each time you play, shade one star in your favorite color!

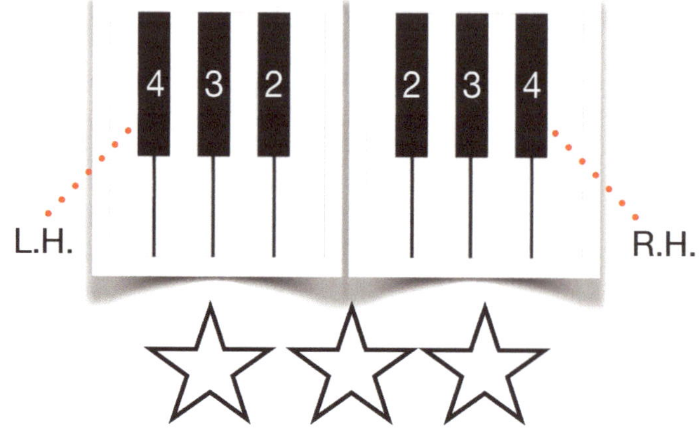

Play this piece 3 times and color a star each time you play!

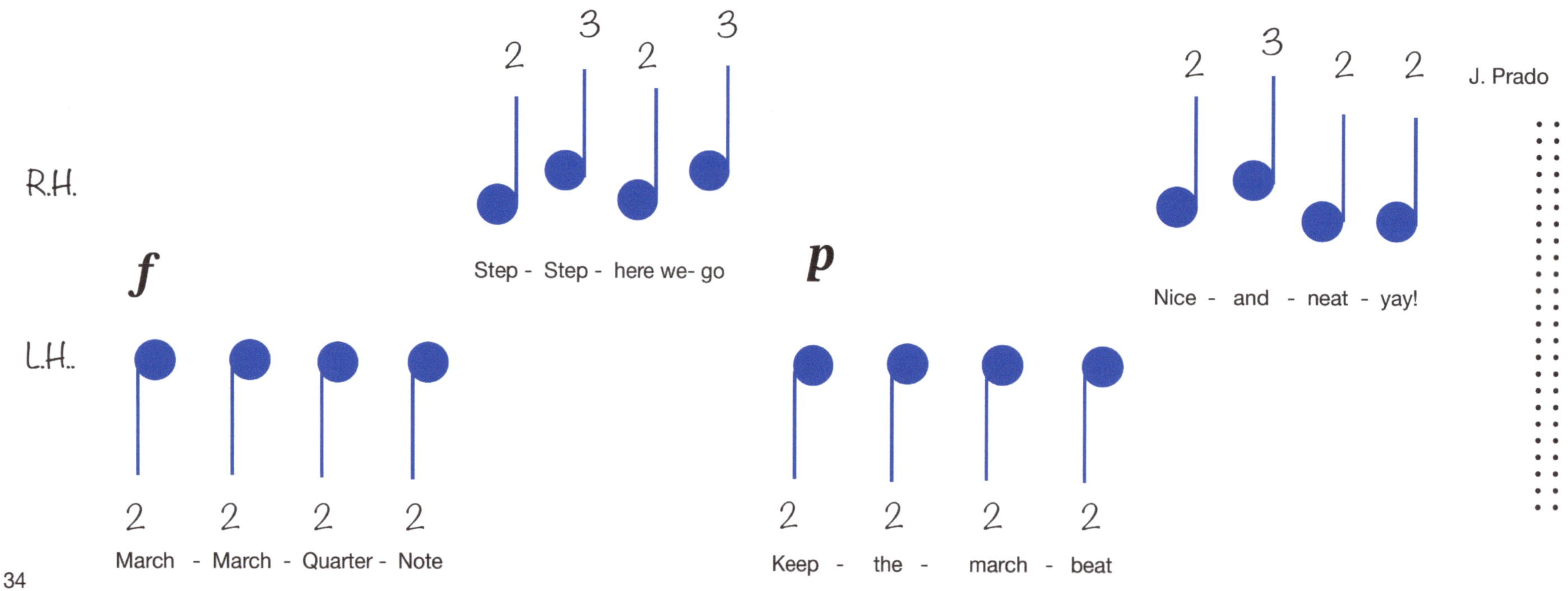

J. Prado

R.H.

3 3
2   2

Step - Step - here we- go

2 3 2 2

Nice - and - neat - yay!

f

L.H.

2 2 2 2

March - March - Quarter - Note

p

2 2 2 2

Keep - the - march - beat

Tick-Tock Rhythm

For this song:

- The teacher will first play and sing the song for the student.
- Tap on the closed piano lid using the correct hand and count the beats aloud.
- Using the the correct fingers on both hands practice the movement one hand at the time on the closed lid of the piano.
- Use the group of two black keys in the middle of the piano, using fingers 2 and 3 on R.H, and for L.H use a lower group of two black keys using fingers 2 and 3
- Add dynamics!
- Each time you play it, please shade one star using your favorite color.

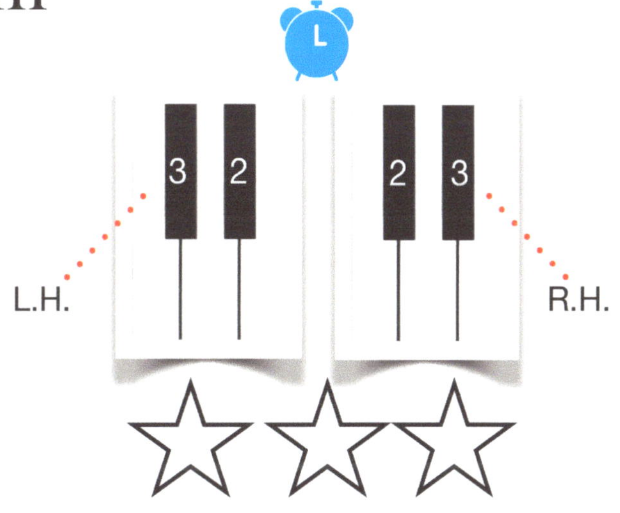

Play this piece 3 times and color a star each time you play!

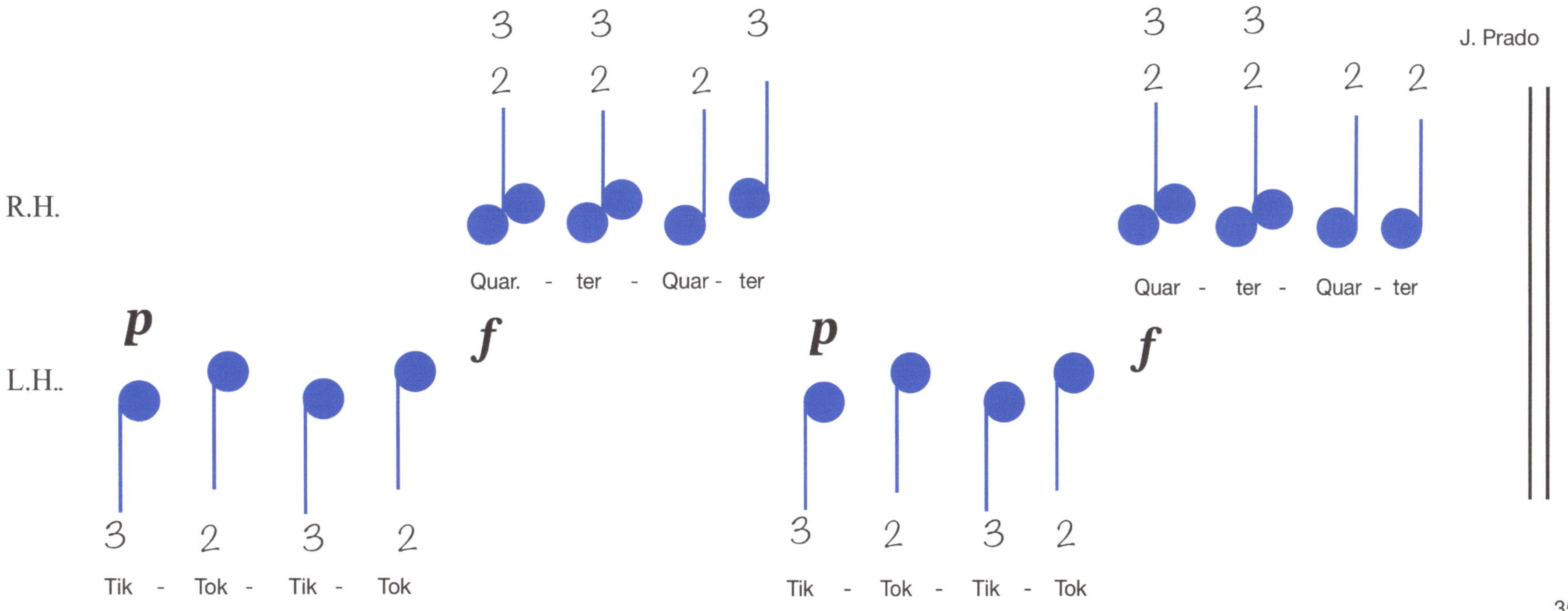

J. Prado

R.H.

3 3 3
2 2 2

Quar. - ter - Quar - ter

3 3
2 2 2 2

Quar - ter - Quar - ter

p   *f*   *p*   *f*

L.H..

3 2 3 2

Tik - Tok - Tik - Tok

3 2 3 2

Tik - Tok - Tik - Tok

Jungle Drum Fun

For this song:

- The teacher will first play and sing the song for the student.
- Start by tapping on the closed piano lid with the correct hand and count the beats out loud as you go.
- Using the correct fingers, practice the hand movements one at a time on the closed piano lid:
- Use the group of three black keys in the middle of the piano, using fingers 2, 3, and 4 on L.H, and for R.H use the a higher group of three black keys using fingers 2, 3, and 4.
- Add dynamics!
- Each time you practice, color in one star with your favorite color to track your progress.

Play this piece 3 times and color a star each time you play!

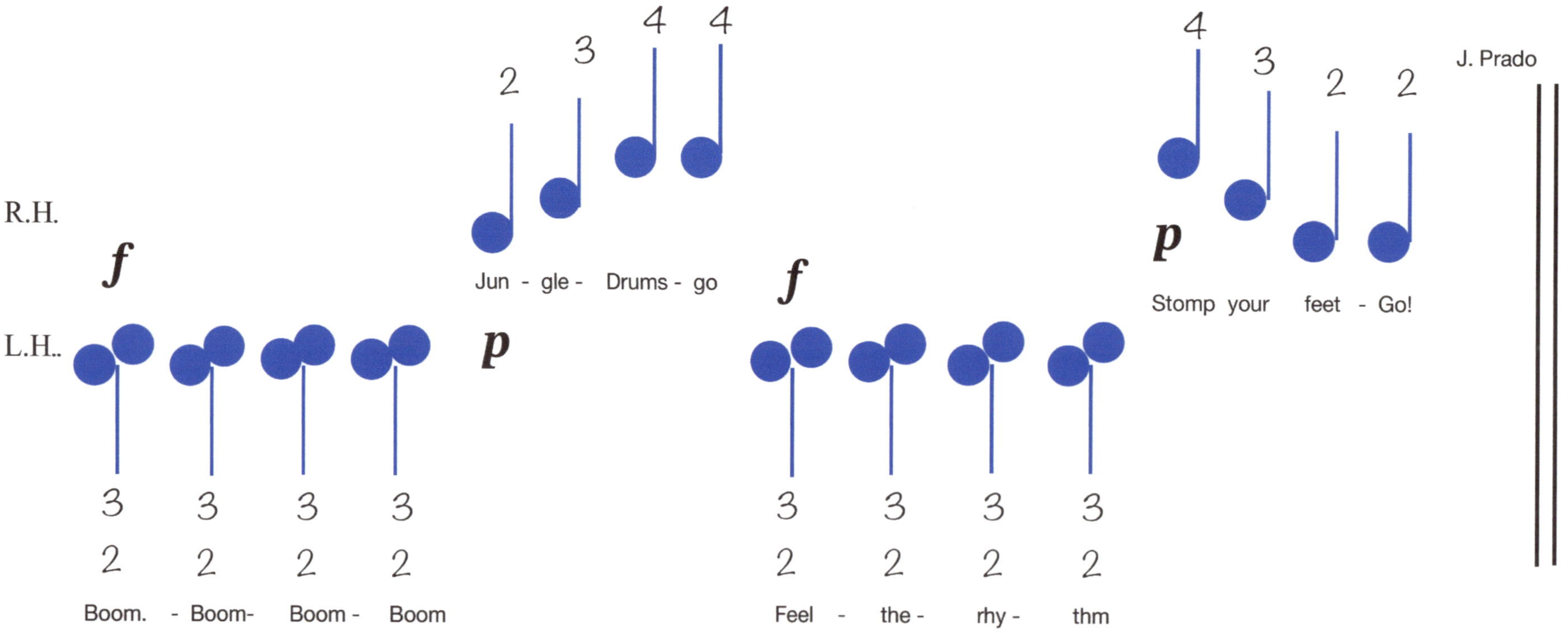

The Prado Piano Method™ - Jennifer Prado

Lest's Compose a Song

For this song:

- Let's compose a piece together using the finger numbers 2, 3, and 4.
- First, pick which hand will start.
- Write the quarter notes and corresponding numbers for the Right Hand (R.H.) and Left Hand (L.H.). Remember to add dynamics!
- Would you like to add some lyrics?
- Trace the double bar line
- Let's play the song!

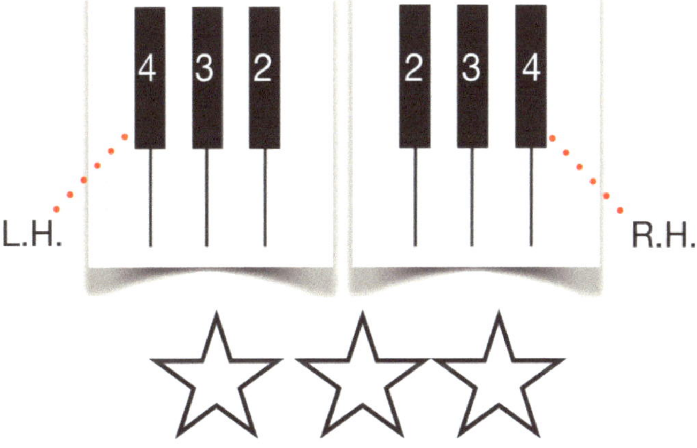

Play this piece 3 times and color a star each time you play!

R.H.

L.H.

Rhythm Friends: Half Note

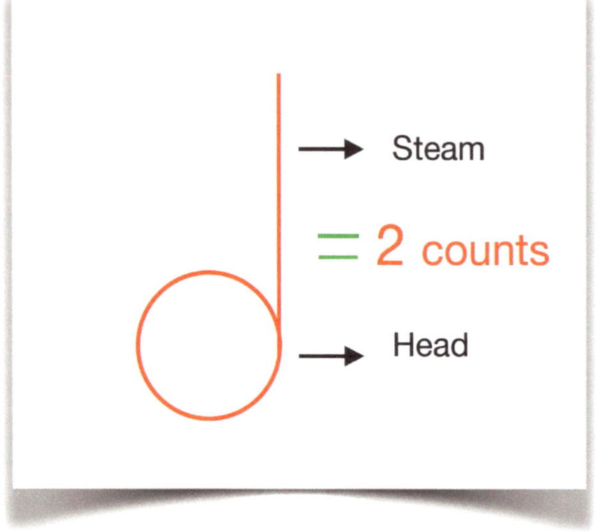

Meet Our Friend, Half Note!

Half Note gets 2 counts or beats. Let's create one together!

- **Make a Circle:** Draw a small circle.
- **Add a Stem:** Draw a straight line extending upward from the right side of the circle
- **Say Hi:** Wave and say "Hi" to your new friend half note!

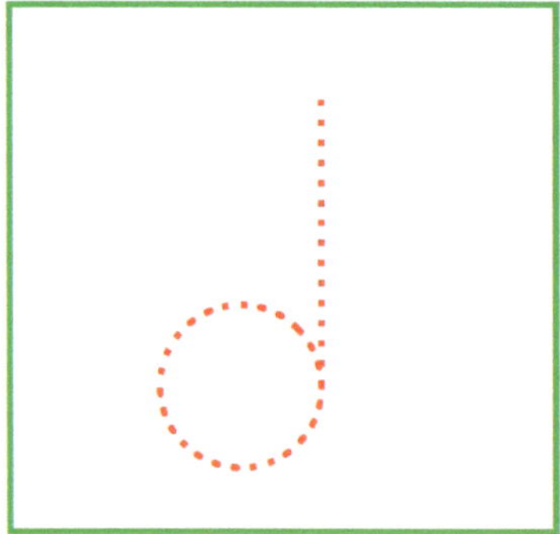
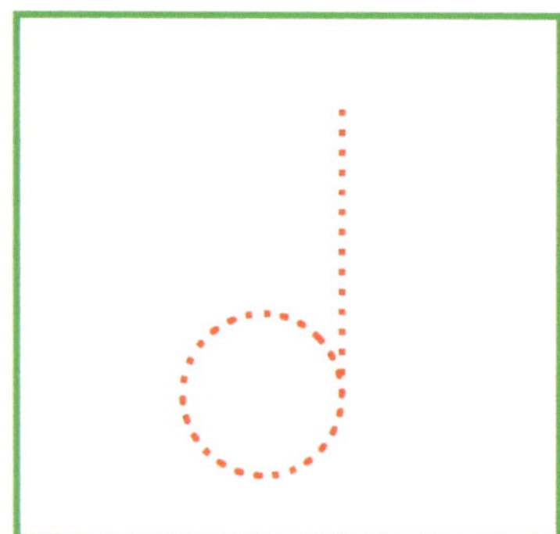
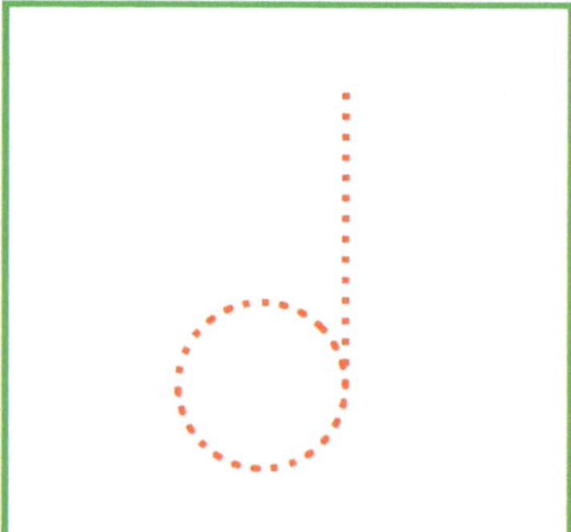

Rhythm Friends: Half Note

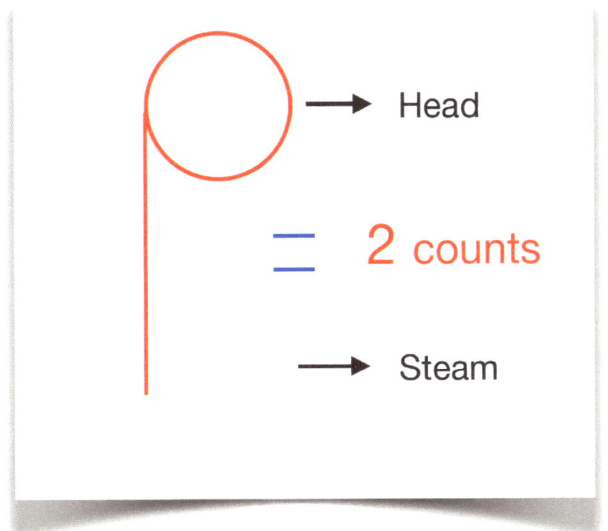

Our friend Half Note can have the stem going up or down. Let's create one with the stem going down!

- **Make a Circle:** Draw a small circle.
- **Add a Stem:** Draw a straight line extending downwards from the circle.
- **Say Hi:** Wave and say "Hi" to your new friend half note!

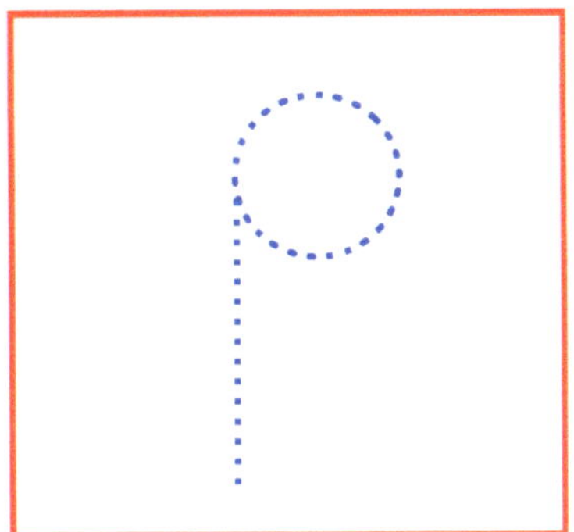
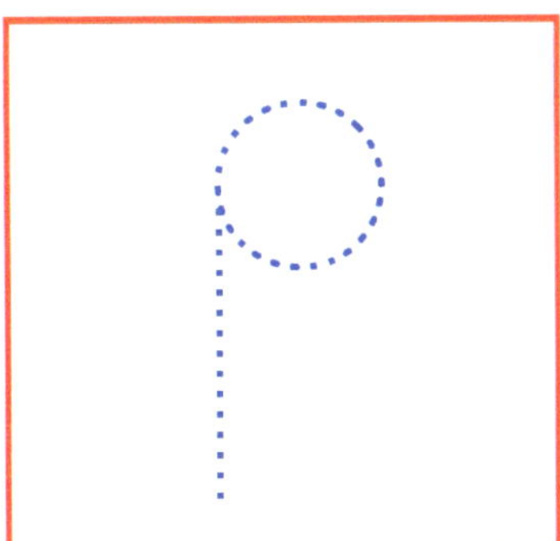
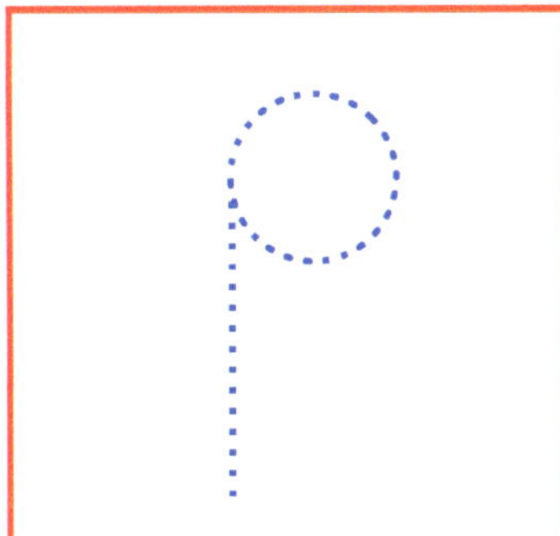

Half Note: Game Time Fun

For this game:

- Tap all the Half Notes on your knees using your right hand (R.H.) or left hand (L.H.), counting **two beats aloud** for each half note. Repeat this three times, increasing speed each time, and shade one star after each round.
- Using your favorite color, circle all the Half Notes with the stem DOWN.

Tap this rhythm 3 times and color a star each time you tap!

Marching Strong

For this piece:

- The teacher will first play and sing the song for the student.
- Tap on the closed piano lid with the correct hand while counting the beats aloud.
- Practice the finger movements for each hand separately on the closed lid.
- Use the group of two black keys in the middle of the piano, using fingers 2, and 3 for your left hand (L.H.) and the group of three black keys for your right hand (R.H.) using fingers 2, 3, and 4.
- Add dynamics!
- Each time you play, shade one star in your favorite color!

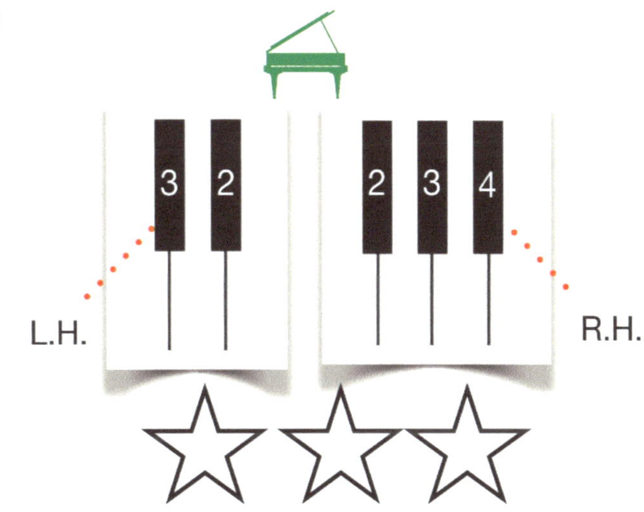

Play this piece 3 times and color a star each time you play!

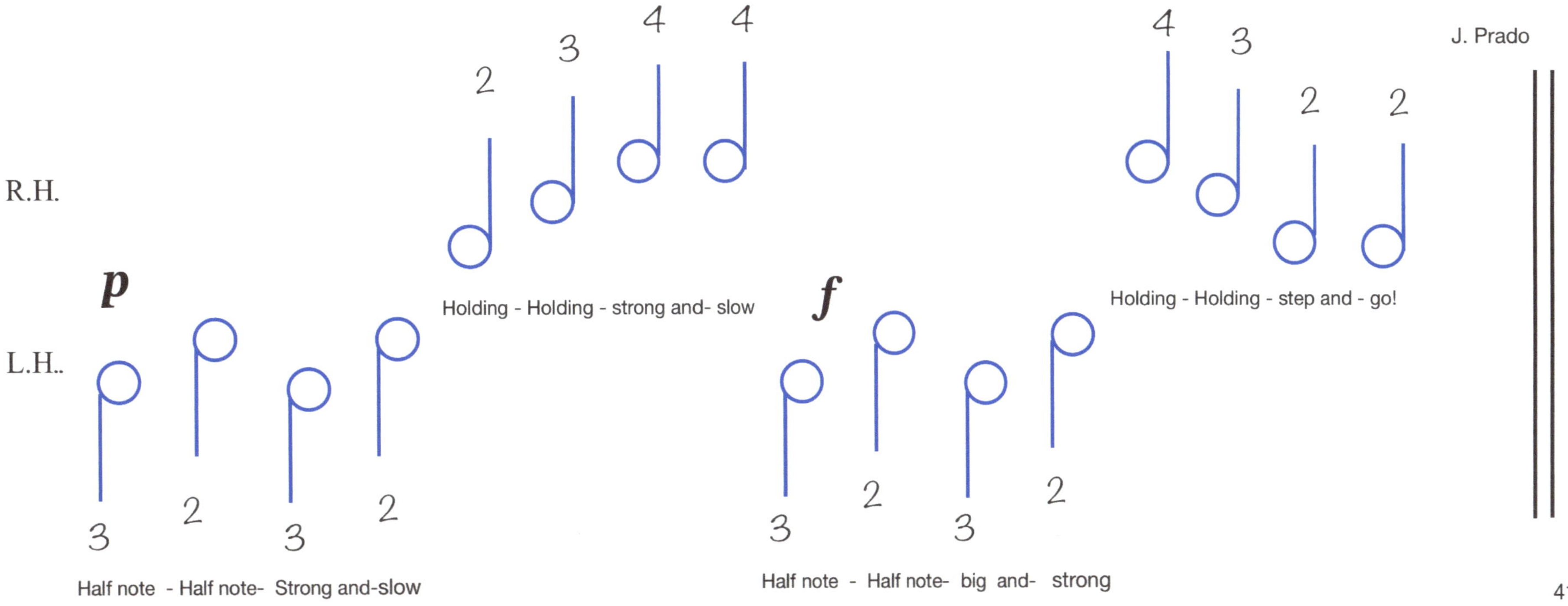

Step and Clap

For this piece:

- The teacher will first play and sing the song for the student.
- Tap the rhythm on your knees with the correct hand while counting the beats aloud (1 and 2 for half notes and 1 for quarter note)
- Practice the finger movements for each hand separately on the closed lid.
- Use the group of two black keys in the middle of the piano, using fingers 2, and 3 for your left hand (L.H.) and a the group of three black keys for your right hand (R.H.) using fingers 2, 3, and 4.
- Add dynamics!
- Each time you play, shade one star in your favorite color!

Play this piece 3 times and color a star each time you play!

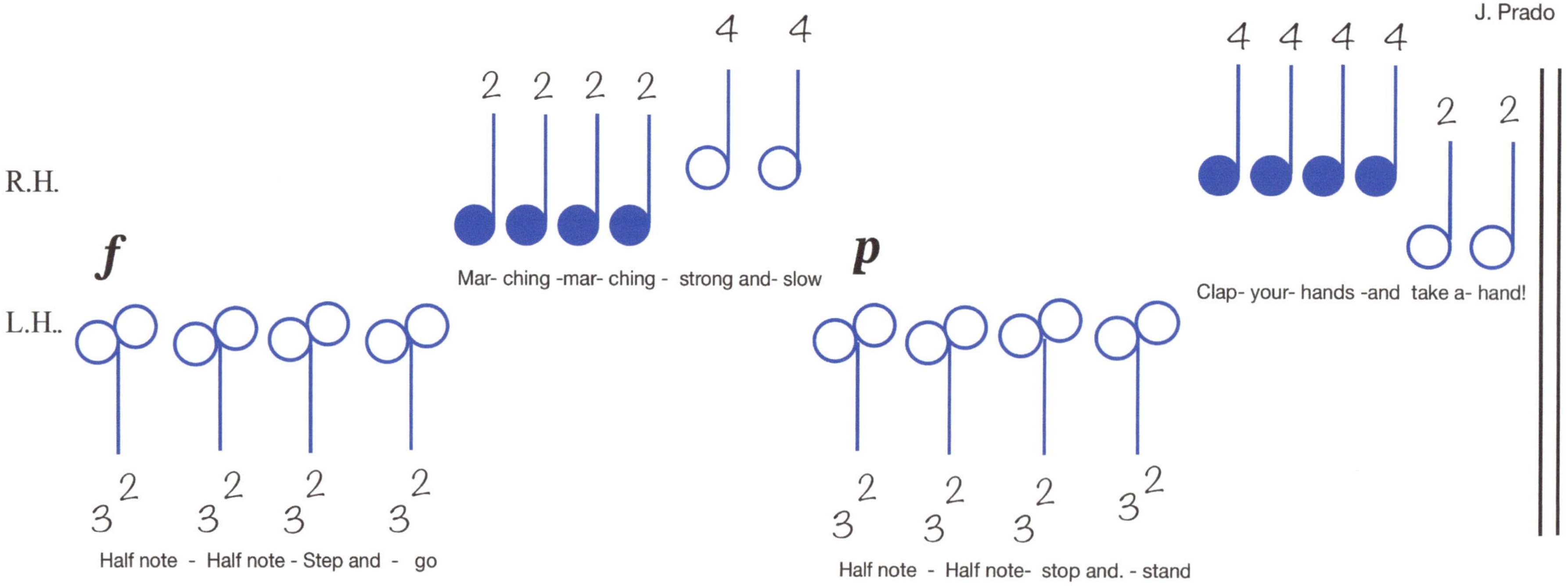

J. Prado

R.H.

L.H..

f

Mar- ching -mar- ching - strong and- slow

Half note - Half note - Step and - go

p

Half note - Half note- stop and. - stand

Clap- your- hands -and take a- hand!

The Prado Piano Method™ - Jennifer Prado

Tiptoe Kitty

For this piece:

- The teacher will first play and sing the song for the student.
- Tap on the closed piano lid with the correct hand while counting the beats aloud.
- Practice the finger movements for each hand separately on the closed lid.
- Use the group of two black keys in the middle of the piano, using fingers 2, and 3 for your left hand (L.H.) and a the group of three black keys for your right hand (R.H.) using fingers 2, 3, and 4.
- Add dynamics!
- Each time you play, shade one star in your favorite color!

3
2
2
3
4
L.H.
R.H.

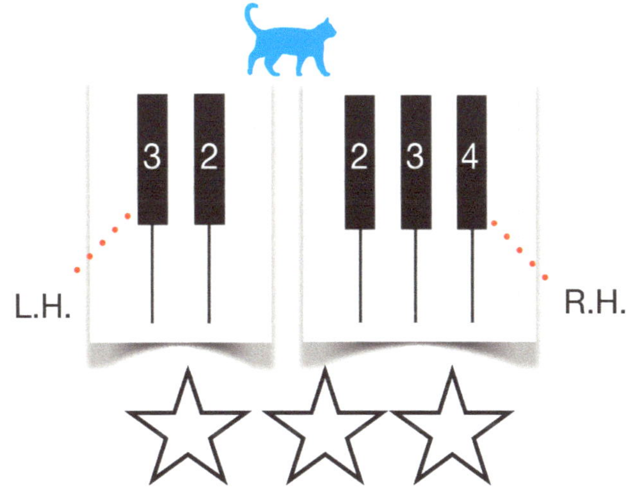

Play this piece 3 times and color a star each time you play!

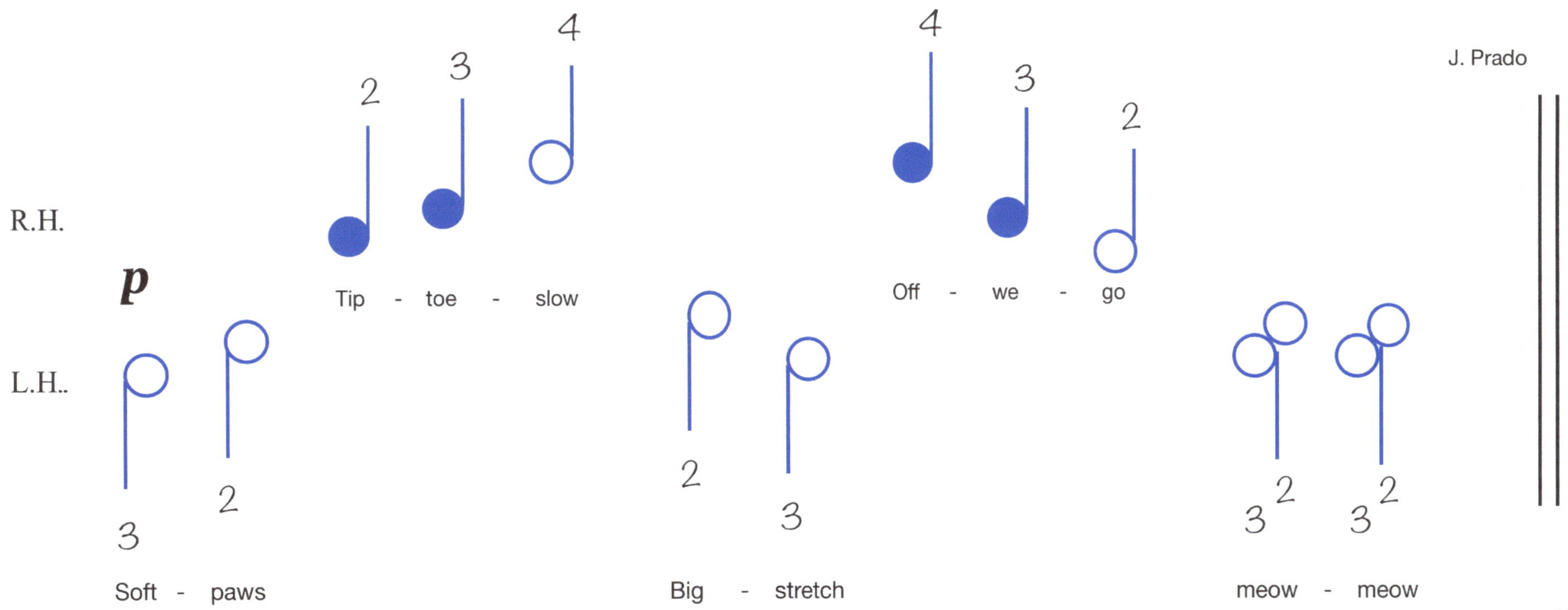

J. Prado
R.H.
L.H..
p
3 2
Soft - paws
2 3 4
Tip - toe - slow
2 3
Big - stretch
4 3 2
Off - we - go
3 2 3 2
meow - meow

Lest's Compose a Song

For this song:

- Let's compose a piece together using finger numbers 2, and 3 in the L.H, and 2, 3, and 4 in the R.H.
- First, pick which hand will start.
- Then, write a combination of quarter and half notes along with the corresponding finger numbers for both R.H. and L.H. Add dynamics!
- Would you like to add some lyrics?
- Trace the double bar line
- Let's play the song!

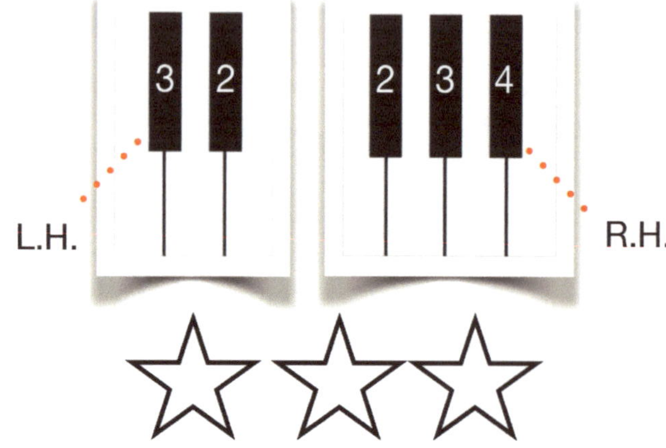

Play this piece 3 times and color a star each time you play!

R.H.

L.H.

Certificate of Achievement

This certifies that ________________________ has successfully completed
(Student Name)

Preparatory Level – Book A of *The Prado Piano Method*™. You've reached the end of Book A—

wonderful work!

You have learned new rhythms, explored finger numbers, played fun songs, and taken your first steps in understanding how music works. Each time you sat at the piano, you grew into a stronger and more confident musician.

Remember… every great pianist begins exactly where you are now—one note at a time.

Keep practicing, keep exploring, and most of all… keep having fun!

Your musical adventure continues in Book B.

See you at the piano!

Teacher's Signature: __________________   **Date:** __________

The Prado Piano Method™

The Prado Piano Method™

A joyful and structured approach to early piano learning.

The **Prado Piano Method™** introduces young beginners to the world of music through engaging activities, creative pieces, and a carefully guided step-by-step progression. Designed for children ages 4–6, this preparatory series helps students build strong musical foundations while discovering the joy of playing the piano.

Through rhythm games, note-reading exercises, creative activities, and beginner piano pieces, students develop essential skills in:

Music theory
Sight reading
Ear training
Technique
Piano repertoire

The method encourages children to clap, sing, draw, write, compose, and play—creating a well-rounded and playful musical learning experience.

Perfect for private lessons, music schools, and home learning, **The Prado Piano Method™** nurtures confidence, creativity, and a lifelong love of music.

Jennifer Prado

Founder of Prado Music Academy
Creator of The Prado Piano Method™

www.pradomusicacademy.com